A Little Book o

Values and Virtues for a More Successful Life

Ms. Santone,
I hope you find this informative, insightful, and motivational.

Wil Brower
1/6/23

Wilbur L. Brower, Ph. D.

ALSO BY DR. WILBUR L. BROWER

Defining Your Success—You Decide What You Want Out of Life (2013)

The Seven C's of Success—Developing the Attributes, Attitudes and Behaviors to Achieve All You Want Out of Life (2013)

When Justice Calls—A novel (2013)

Of Life, Love and Learning—Selected Poems and Educational Raps, Rhythms and Rhymes (2012)

English Grammar and Writing Made Easy—Learn to Communicate More Accurately, Clearly and Concisely (2012)

Traffic Signs on the Road of Life (2012), co-authored with Cynthia Brower

Me Teacher, Me...Please!—Observation and Thoughts about Parents, Students, Teachers and the Teaching-Learning Process (2001)

Personal Care Journal-The Adult Years (2000, co-authored)

Visit the Author's Page:
http://tinyurl.com/ckw5ms8

A Little Book of Big Principles

Comments about *A Little Book of big Principles*

So much of how we experience life is determined not only by the nature of our interactions with others, but also by the choices we make or fail to make regarding others. In our personal lives and our professional decisions, we have more control and influence over our lives than we are often led to believe.

We have no choice about our economic position or social standing when we enter into the world, but we do have some choices about what we do with our lives once we are here. We can choose where, when and how we expend our energies to change our economic outcomes and social standing; and change or formulate our relationships with significant and insignificant others. This is easier to do with a set of guiding principles and A Little Book of Big Principles—Values and Virtues for a More Successful Life instructs us on how to do it.

These principles can serve as a voice of conscience during times of uncertainty; as a motivating force when giving up seems like the only way out; and as a beacon of light during times of despair. They articulate what some people know intuitively and act on instinctively. These principles will equip the reader with the know-how and tools to face and conquer many of life's challenges.

Copyright © 2012 by Wilbur L. Brower, Ph.D.

Library of Congress Control Number: 2012919651

Brower, Wilbur L.

1. Motivation 2. Personal/professional development
3. Self-Development 4. Success in Life

Correspondence to the author should be directed to:

Dr. Wilbur L. Brower

P. O. Box 565

Trenton, NC 28585

Cell: (910) 548-0698

E-mail: wlbrower@gmail.com

ISBN: 978-1-6922870-6-1

To my Father and Mother,

who always did what they could

with what they had;

and

To my son Neil,

who wanted to grow up

to be my twin

Acknowledgements

While it has been nearly fifteen years since A Little Book of Big Principles—Values and Virtues for a More Successfully Life was first released, I am still indebted to all the people who helped me to bring the project to fruition, and I owe much to many people who have played vital roles in the development and publication of this revised edition. The resonance that the book had for many people who read it was much more than I had anticipated, and it was their comments about how the book spoke to them personally and changed their lives, along with their desire to share what they learned with others, were the impetus for me to refine, update and re-publish it in print and eBook formats.

I have attempted to digest every comment from numerous unsolicited letters, private conversations with clients, colleagues and students, and voice-mail messages from many people of various backgrounds, and to incorporate their feedback and sentiments into the additional principles. Therefore, I am eternally grateful to all who shared their comments and offered their insights.

I am thankful to Ajmer Singh who took the ideas about the book's presentation and developed some superb samples that I believe capture the essence of its contents. Many thanks to him for the fantastic final design and layout of the contents! I am also thankful to Mrs. Janet Thomas for reviewing the new principles and offering suggestions on phrasing.

I give special thanks to my wife Cynthia Waters-Brower whose initial interest in helping me to market the book eventually led to our getting married three years later. The marketing was sidelined for more than ten years, but it is because of her interest in the application of technology to learning that re-energized me to get the re-write and marketing back on track. I am grateful to her for the enormous amount of time and effort she spent exploring the various publishing formats and options for the book. It is because of her that this edition will be an even greater success.

CONTENTS

PREFACE

Any time is the perfect time to read Wilbur Brower's 'pay it forward', ageless wisdom for creating a fulfilling life. In this updated edition of *A Little Book of Big Principles – Values and Virtues for a More Successful Life*, Wil once again challenges us to identify the importance of managing ourselves and our relationships with others. He invites us to create meaningful lives by our own definitions, not the world's, offering a powerfully, simply and clearly written set of principles that transcend time in their relevance.

What Wil has learned through experience and being a witness to the successes of others, as they have applied these principles, is highly instructive.

Three book sections – *Personal Growth, Interpersonal Relationship, and Professional Development*- are filled with thought-provoking examples of his principles in action. Engaging quotes introducing each principle stimulate us to think *critically* about the narratives that follow.

Each principle reminds us that identifying and refining our talents is the means to living a prosperous and purposeful life. Each narrative links its principle to circumstances that can be personalized to the reader's reality. Each page of narrative reinforces the importance of following our passions and living in the moment.

Through Wil's compassionate voice and life lessons, we are reminded that values learned in childhood play out in our adult lives. So, improving our interactions with others begins with personal insight, self-respect, and a deep appreciation for all humanity. What follows, he suggests, is the acceptance that every person's journey is filled with bumps in the road, providing opportunities for humility and growth – should we choose to take them.

Wil encourages us to analyze the impact of our thinking on our choices and to examine the ways in which our principles support or victimize ourselves and others.

He graciously reminds us that most of us have a sense of what will bring us happiness and success. In fact, when we are asked to do so, we can make long lists of these things. However, it's living our list, with integrity, without fear of rejection or criticism, and with the desire to listen and learn that define the result achieved and the fulfillment we experience.

A Little Book of Big Principles is a keeper. There's much food for thought within its pages. You will see yourself and others from whom your lessons have been gleaned. This book is to be read, re-read, studied and practiced. You will probably write notes in the margins and keep a highlighter nearby. If you want a friend to read it, which you certainly will, buy them a copy. Discuss and share your insights with family, colleagues, children, and friends. Commit to your continuous learning and to supporting those whose lives crisscross yours. Applaud as others experience the 'a-ha' moments that follow positive changes in their thinking and behavior. Most of us are hungry for inspiration – A Little Book of Big Principles provides a banquet!

Mary Stewart-Pellegrini, Ph. D.
Author of Equitychecking: Managing Personal Assumptions to Achieve Organizational Success.

FOREWORD

In today's hectic, fast-forward world, it's far too easy to lose sight of why we're doing what we are and to overlook the powerful potential we all hold to conduct our life differently.

The way we choose to lead our lives is, more than ever, subject to outside pressures. We may, quite naturally, feel overwhelmed or discouraged until we discover that the strongest defense against negative influences requires staying true to the best of human instincts: optimism, realism, kindness and honesty.

The reality is that most of us have precious little time to discover, or rediscover, our own inner wisdom—to think, to reflect, and to sort out priorities for our personal and professional lives.

A Little Book of Big Principles offers a road map for opening up new options when you feel stuck, for helping you make the right choices when you find yourself at a cross-road, for turning over a new leaf when you've hit some rough spots or encountered some road blocks.

You'll find this book of great comfort if you seek a new vision for how to lead your daily life.

You'll open this book when you need to find new workable solutions to those old problems which never seem to go away.

You'll give this book to a friend who needs a bit of inspiration and a fresh perspective on how to face life's challenges—large and small.

You'll read *A Little Book of Big Principles* because you are determined to reach your fullest potential in every aspect of your life.

As Wil Brower recommends strategies for casting aside behaviors which are self-defeating and rejecting attitudes which are self-limiting, he offers positive messages of hope and inspiration. If you stumble, dare to dream; if you're uncertain, dare to take risks; if you fear failure, dare to challenge yourself. With the limitless reach of the human spirit, there is no good reason not to achieve a rewarding, productive and balanced life.

As a lifelong learner himself, Wil offers wise counsel for finding meaningful work, for developing rewarding relationships, and for feeling at peace with ourselves.

Don't allow yourself to become a victim, he stresses. Take responsibility for your own actions and take charge of your own journey.

In *A Little Book of Big Principles*, Wil Brower conveys the humanity, generosity and compassion with which he leads his own life. As a mentor for his own son, for high school students, for individuals and for corporations, Wil conveys the unlimited potential that lies within all of us. He shares with us the strength and wisdom of the beliefs that he himself practices by actions and example.

The generosity of his spirit, the power of his convictions and the strength of his moral character are the forces behind Wil's longtime efforts to create a principled, caring and decent society where every individual is valued and where differences are celebrated.

In his powerful and inspirational voice, Wil offers a moral framework for helping us reach our finest promise as individuals and as members of an increasingly interdependent society.

Deborah J. Swiss, Ph. D.
Author of Women Breaking Through and Women and the Work/Family Dilemma

INTRODUCTION

It is generally accepted that the "hard" sciences are built on a set of universal principles. These principles lay the foundation for the discipline or branch of knowledge. The way in which the principles are applied will determine the results. There are also principles in the "soft" sciences, by which we usually mean human behavior or human relations. How we apply these principles will also determine the quality of the results we are likely to get.

The principles noted here are collections of mother wit or commonsense that pertains to how we manage ourselves and our interactions with others. I first wrote them to explain some of the dynamics of human relationships, but they grew into a representative sampling of expressions that individuals found personally insightful and professionally meaningful. These principles spoke volumes to individuals about their own behaviors and the behaviors of others. They ended up on refrigerator doors, bedroom mirrors and office walls as constant reminders and personal motivators for individuals determined to take charge of their lives and their careers.

Because of the popularity of the principles, I was encouraged by colleagues and friends to expand upon the ideas and concepts and to put them into the form of a little book. By no means are the principles all-inclusive, but I hope they will give the reader "some food for thought" and a different perspective about her or his own behaviors and the behaviors of others.

PERSONAL GROWTH AND DEVELOPMENT

A Little Book of Big Principles Values and Virtues for a More Successful Life

Take personal responsibility for your actions and inactions.

I t's easy to blame others when things don't go the way you want them to or the way you think they should. And if they don't go well because of something you did or failed to do, you may try to blame someone else and then assume that you are off the hook. But all the blaming in the world will not absolve you of the role you played. If you give up your responsibilities concerning choices you should make and action you should take, you have to accept the results, no matter what they are.

You will also have to face the fact that you did nothing to achieve your desired results. If you take inappropriate actions and make bad choices, you have to live with the results. Blaming others may provide a temporary sense of relief, but ultimately the burden will rest on your shoulders.

Be responsible for your actions, and you will be your own master.

If you don't believe in yourself, no one else will.

Numerous people and circumstances can make you doubt yourself and your abilities. A steady diet of disbelief from people who are significant in your life and from circumstances that tend to invalidate you will eventually fill you with self-doubt. These feelings can cause you to act, talk and walk with little or no confidence, to develop a maybe-I'm-not-deserving attitude, to hesitate when you are given an opportunity to show what you can do, and to give up easily when faced with a challenge.

All of these behaviors will reflect a belief that says, "I'm not worthy of being respected and taken seriously. I'm not strong. I will not persevere. I do not have a strong desire to excel and to succeed. I will not stand up for what I believe."

Show that you believe in yourself, and then others will believe in you.

It is from our greatest challenges that we often discover our true strengths.

Challenges are part of everyday living. They can test your emotional, intellectual and physical well-being, often preventing you from reaching your true potential—if you let them. If you give up when you're faced with them, you are unlikely to succeed at or excel in many of the things you would like to accomplish. However, if you learn to persist and persevere when challenged, you're more likely to become stronger from the experience.

You'll also gain insights about yourself, your capabilities and your real potential. You can learn that you really are strong, you can endure, and that minor setbacks in life give you all the more reason not to give up or give in to self-doubt. Challenges you've overcome show you and others just how capable you are, and they give you real evidence of your true strengths.

Don't go around picking up rocks and putting them in your wagon— they get heavy real soon.

L ife poses many challenges for us; often we call them burdens. We can blame all of these burdens, or unpleasant experiences, or negative perceptions on how we are treated, or on one or more of our personal attributes or characteristics, such as our gender, race, or religion. As a result, it's easy to become paranoid, accumulate more and more of these burdens and end up making ourselves miserable.

What's just as true is that if you expect such burdens and look for them, you are sure to find them. Moreover, you will find in every interaction and comment an intentional slight, putdown or slap because of whom you are, whether any slight or putdown was ever intended. Ultimately, you will feel that you have the weight of the world upon your shoulders and not know why, and this feeling will contribute to a belief that you lack control, or that your life is out of control.

Ignore those rocks; they don't need you to give them a ride.

If you don't think and act like a victim, you won't be one.

Throughout human history, many people have been control. These oppressed individuals have subjugated to those in power and been mentally and physically abused, tortured and led to believe that they could not control their actions. In the face of amputations, decapitations, genocide and mass murders, the powerless have been conditioned to become helpless and to yield their fate to the powerful, who have controlled and have been quick to use the devices and weapons of destruction.

Under such conditions, the vast majority of the powerless has become debilitated, dysfunctional and immobile, and has slipped into a state of disorder from which they find it nearly impossible to extricate themselves. Their goal has been simply to survive from day to day and to escape the wrath of the powerful. Although in more recent times the degree of man's inhumanity to man has decreased, the residuals of it are ever-present. Thus, the belief that one is helpless, and the feelings of helplessness and lack of control are socialized into succeeding generations.

While there may be many negative social cues that attempt to invalidate you as an individual, to diminish your efforts and accomplishments, and to erode your self-confidence, these can be actual results ONLY if you allow them to be. Any negative self-images and self-effacing behaviors you exhibit are not inherent characteristics, but only reflections of your level of acceptance of the prevailing environmental forces.

Wilbur L. Brower, Ph. D.

When you change your attitude, you can change you life.

It is often said that attitude is everything. To be sure, your attitude reveals how you feel about yourself and determines how others will interact with you. Remember that your behavior is driven by your attitude, which is the essence of who you really are. Most people would prefer not to deal with someone who has a "nasty attitude," or who constantly complains about everything without offering suggestions about possible improvements, or who finds ways to belittle or denigrate others, or who is impossible to work with.

If you have a negative attitude, you can make yourself, as well as others with whom you come in contact, very miserable. People will avoid you, steer clear and closely monitor their interactions with you. Finally, negative attitudes make you unapproachable; you lose the benefit of candor, genuine interpersonal interactions, open and honest communications, and the willingness of others to show concern.

Someone once said, "Your attitude will determine your altitude." I agree.

If you have no goals, you're like a ship without a rudder

A rudder is a device used to steer an aircraft, a boat, hovercraft, ship, or submarine, directing the course the traveler wants to take. Without a rudder, the traveler is taken wherever the waters or winds are going.

The most important step toward self-mastery is to establish a clear plan about where you want to go and how you are going to get there. Then act, talk and walk with unyielding determination and purpose. Remember that your mission is to set your eye on a target on the horizon, plot your course, set your rudder, and hoist your sail, fully believing that you will reach it. Navigate yourself in the belief that you control your own destiny. You will be beset by high winds and stormy seas; but, learn to use such adversities to your advantage.

Maintain your course in spite of all the distractions around you. Don't be like those people who just float along in life, going wherever circumstances happen to take them. They have no real purpose and mission. They wash ashore easily or drift into stagnant waters regularly. They cannot make headway in rough waters, and they are at the mercy of rough seas. They rarely optimize their potential or accomplish in life all that they desire.

Stop procrastinating; establish a plan and set your goals.

The quality of our lives is determined by the choices we make.

Generally, in life, we have the power to choose from a range of options available to us. There is, for the most part, free-will. However, there are some circumstances that are forced upon us, such as mandatory education until a certain age. While we are exposed to the opportunity to acquire an education in this instance, it is our choice to take advantage of that opportunity because it will benefit us or to squander it because we might think the education is for somebody else.

Whatever choice we make, there are associated consequences—good, bad or otherwise. We have to be informed, insightful or intuitive enough to anticipate the short-term and long-term consequences of our choices. We cannot blame others for the choices we make, especially if the options are clear and convincing. If we make wise choices, we benefit from them daily; if we make bad choices, we are likely to be harmed by them for what will probably feel like an eternity.

You don't manage time;
you can only manage yourself during
the time you have.

Time is a universal concept; and it does not discriminate. We all have exactly the same amount of time. However, while some people are able to accomplish a lot within the amount they have, others accomplish almost nothing. What accounts for the difference? It is not intelligence, gender, race or religion. To a degree, it may be the way one is socialized. But, ultimately, it has to do with the individual and the way he or she "thinks" about the results and the value of one's efforts, and then how he or she follows through.

Some people go through life with commitment, dedication, focus and a singleness of purpose; they are determined to accomplish what they set out to do. They are organized and well-managed because they manage themselves. It is not surprising that they are more likely to achieve their goals, and they appear to achieve them with great economy and facility. They tend to focus on the results they want and not on the obstacles that are ever-present.

Conversely, there are people who have no idea what they want. They often don't like their current circumstances, but they make little or no effort to change them. They are willing to complain and blame their dilemma on the world-at-large rather than to set about determining what they want and going after it. Often, they are very bitter people because they feel that life has dealt them a "bad hand;" or they feel that there is never enough time to get anything done. They refuse to take charge and get things done—so they do nothing.

Wilbur L. Brower, Ph. D.

*Don't use others' prejudices as excuses
for not achieving your goals;
their prejudices are all the more
reason for you to succeed.*

Many people dislike and even hate others without knowing anything about them, and they can do so solely because of their language, physical characteristics, race, religion or sexual orientation. They are engaged in dangerous and destructive stereotyping, ascribing to others all the worst characteristics of a particular group, or that can be found in any group. They inevitably project an air of arrogance and superiority. It takes a lot not to be drawn into their mindless little game, which attempts to say, "I am better than you." If you lower yourself to play their game, you will be no better than they.

However, if you observe such people more closely, you will discover that their attitudes and behaviors are convenient devices to camouflage the realities of their own mediocrity and their doubts about their feeling of superiority. Indeed, at close range, you will find them to be ignorant and woefully ill-informed. If you choose to acknowledge their comments or presence—and sometimes it is best not to—it should be with the intentions of educating them and leaving them with something profound to think about.

Don't take their "arrows of hate" and thrust them into your own heart. You don't have the problem; they do. You have to keep your eyes on your goals, remain fleet of foot, become more resolved, and move on.

The world owes you nothing; what you get out of life is in proportion to what you put into it.

L ife is not always fair; nobody ever said it would be. We all suffer many disappointments, heartbreaks, letdowns, and setbacks. That's just the way life is. It's very easy to look at another person's seemingly pleasant situation and complain about the unfair hand you may think you've been dealt. However, you can't give your life back and ask for another. Complaining doesn't help, and wallowing in self-pity doesn't change anything. Blaming everyone else for your circumstances won't arouse much sympathy.

In fact, very few people really care why you may not have accomplished all that you want to in life or why you haven't acquired all that you think you deserve. However, more people than you might think are willing to help those whom they believe are willing to try. Whatever the hand you've been dealt, you still are given an opportunity to play it to the best of your ability.

Don't sit and wait, believing that someone is going to play your hand for you, or that someone will be willing to exchange their "good" hand for yours. The fact is, if you don't try to play it, you'll never see opportunities before your eyes that can help you to score, and score big, regardless of the kind of hand you think you have been dealt.

You cannot let your current circumstances define who you are and what you are capable of becoming.

Many unfair and unfortunate circumstances may befall us through no-fault of our own. They can be the early death of a parent; birth into a family that has never considered financial or personal successes as viable options; injuries sustained from an automobile accident; or the breakup of a marriage. We may have no control over these circumstances, but we, nevertheless, cannot allow them to prevent us from pursuing goals that are likely to give us emotional, financial and social wellbeing. Such circumstances should not automatically place us on the lowest rung of the emotional, financial and social ladders of life. We cannot allow them to limit our aspirations, choices or motivation. We cannot let these circumstances force us onto a track leading to apathy, mediocrity and self-destruction.

We have to define ourselves much higher and to see our possibilities more valuable than those circumstances, and not allow them to keep us from achieving the fullness of our humanity and all that it entails. Ultimately, such circumstances are only minor inconveniences encountered on the road to personal fulfillment and success.

We have to find the courage to look beyond our current circumstances and find the star pointing us toward our true destiny.

"Manage" your own expectations— positive and negative. Don't let others do it for you.

"The difference between a lady and a flower girl is not how she behaves, but how she's treated." From Pygmalion

I n George Bernard Shaw's play Pygmalion (1912)—the movie version was "My Fair Lady"—Eliza Doolittle explained a very sophisticated concept in a very simple way. In essence, the character Eliza observes that if a flower girl is treated like a flower girl, she will always be a one; but if she is treated like a lady, she will "become" one. In the same way, others' expectations about your behavior and performance can have a profound effect on you. Likewise, how people in authority or superior positions treat you is influenced by what they expect of you.

The danger comes when people may have low or negative expectations of you for reasons such as your education, family background, gender, race or religion. And if you're not careful, you may fulfill their low or negative expectations, in effect making the false information about you become true. You may also become motivated to perform or behave in a certain way because you believe that you will be better off by doing what seems to be expected of you. Such thinking leads to a downward spiral where you allow your behavior to be somebody else's property.

Develop high and positive expectations for yourself, and learn to manage them.

Do not become consumed by material possessions; they are not substitutes for accomplishments, attitude, competence, confidence, contributions, and knowledge.

Many media outlets in society try to convince us that fads and fashions make us the individuals we want and need to be. They tell us that fads and fashions will give us feelings of self-worth and belonging and will increase our self-esteem. But fads and fashions are ephemeral and fleeting—they disappear just as quickly as they appear. They focus on material possessions and styles that make individuals cultural stooges.

If we accept the notion that fads and fashions define us, we are likely to focus all of our attention, expend all of our energy and spend all of our money on whatever the popular culture says is important, and we will do it whenever the popular culture says to do it. Then the search for self becomes a neverending process; meanwhile, those who control and manipulate the popular culture are getting very rich from marketing bogus products that are not substitutes for self-esteem and self-worth.

If we buy in and accept their agenda, we are likely to become financially, socially and spiritually bankrupt from squandering all of our resources chasing elusive dreams.

We find the best of who we are within ourselves because of what we do and how we do it.

If we are lost in life, the best way to find ourselves is through serving others.

I t is common for us never to find or to lose sight of our true purpose in life; and it is quite ironic for excesses to contribute to this malady. If we succumb to this condition, developing a passion for anybody or anything outside of our selfish interests becomes difficult to do. Our time, talents and resources will be squandered and wasted; and we will be oblivious to all of the human needs and suffering facing us at every turn. We will be consumed by self-adoration, self-importance and self-indulgence; and we'll have difficulty finding the compassion and humility to see the humanity in others and to find within ourselves the capacity to serve. However, when we learn to serve others selflessly, we are more likely to find and to enhance our own humanity and, in the process, discover our true purpose.

If you can't find peace and happiness within yourself, you're not likely to get it from others.

I t is easy to believe that others are responsible for your happiness and that if you surround yourself with people that you care about, you will be happy. It is also easy to believe that the more material things you own, the happier you will be. But the truth is that you are responsible for your own happiness; others can only add to it if they choose to. Material things add nothing to your happiness; they can only temporarily influence your state of mind.

Very few worthwhile things in life are accomplished without dedication, pain, purpose and sacrifice.

Many people expect to sail through life on luck. They spend little time planning how to succeed. Some do in fact "luck out." They acquire more than they ever dreamed of, but what they acquire are possessions. Because they know that they "lucked out" and that their individual efforts had little, if anything, to do with their "success," their feelings about that success become short-lived. Not long after the novelty of it wears off, disaster often strikes.

In spite of their material possessions, they often feel like failures, and they can become very miserable and obnoxious people. To compensate for these feelings of failure, they often flaunt their "success" and eventually squander it. Ultimately, they realize that all the money and material possessions they luck upon will not give them a true sense of achievement, because they have not earned any of it through the power of their own efforts.

Use every "failure" as a learning experience, not as an excuse to give up.

Without risk, there is no growth. Without challenges, your capacity is not tested. But risks and challenges also inevitably involve some less-than-successful results. Unfortunately, these results are often labeled "failures" that others may interpret as a statement about you and not about the results. If you internalize these "failures," you may decide to give up and not try very hard again because you may become consumed with a fear of failure.

Fear is the psychological pain that accompanies change, challenges, and risks. To avoid that fear, some individuals come to believe that they must play it safe, so they won't have to think about the possibility of "failure." Thus, they lose sight of the fact that life is a risk, and they live a fool's paradise, comfortable in the belief that they are safe. But not taking risks is the surest way to lose. That's because there is a valuable lesson in every result, whether it is successful or unsuccessful. To find it, you must reflect and search within yourself, especially after a less-than-successful outcome.

Holding on to missed opportunities keeps us from seeing and acting on the next opportunities.

When you fail to capitalize on or take advantage of opportunities when they are available to you, they rarely, if ever, present themselves to you again. When you sit around thinking and talking about what could have been, should have been or would have been, you're living in the past, creating a fantasy that is unlikely to resemble the current or future reality.

If you don't learn anything from the missed opportunities, it gains you nothing. We also have to reason that maybe the missed opportunities were not your opportunities. They could have been blessings in disguise. So, dwelling on and trying to hold on to them is unlikely to change anything. The best that you can hope for is that you learned something from them; you then must turn your attention to the opportunities currently staring you in the face, or are coming in your direction in unsuspecting ways.

If you're busy trying to hold on to missed opportunities, you're likely to miss other opportunities.

Growth and development is a never-ending journey, not a final destination.

We are all born lacking knowledge and having few capabilities. How we subsequently develop is influenced by many factors. What we ultimately achieve in life has more to do with how we optimize whatever innate attributes we have, not on how many we have. If we see our optimal development ending at some terminal point or specific place in time, or if we believe that it is limited by money, we will never become the person we are capable of becoming.

If we believe that we are all-knowing because of what we presently know, we have effectively shut ourselves off from the vast reservoirs of knowledge just beyond the horizon. We may believe that development and knowledge are finite and that we have an abundance of both, but the truly knowledgeable, wise person realizes how little she or he actually knows.

PERSONAL GROWTH AND DEVELOPMENT

Thus, the constant search for knowledge and self-improvement should become the super-ordinate goals that act as driving forces in our life. If we don't develop and acquire new knowledge and larger understandings, we will atrophy and lose ground in an increasingly complex and technologically-oriented society that is constantly changing. Resting on past achievements, stale knowledge and former successes is a formula for disappointments in the future.

It is better to have education and knowledge and not need it, than to need it and not have it.

I have often asked, "How much education does one need?" That is a very difficult question to answer for several reasons. First, education is such an encompassing concept that it is difficult to answer. Secondly, people often equate education with a certificate, a diploma, a degree, or the number of letters after a name. But there are many well-educated people who have no certificate, degree or letters after their name.

Conversely, some individuals have all the trappings of education, such as degrees and letters, but are, in fact, very poorly educated, if not actually uneducated. To be sure, education is an ongoing process, which cannot be measured by degrees and letters. Education is a lifelong pursuit with no final date or defined outcome, because life's demands are constantly changing.

Moreover, we have an almost unlimited capacity to learn. In fact, the fascinating and interesting thing about knowledge is that no matter how much we acquire, we never reach a saturation point. Therefore, to the question: "How...?" my answer is: It is better to have education and knowledge and not need it than to need it and not have it.

Review all of the Personal Growth and Development Principles and list at least five that had personal meaning and significance for you. Write what the Principle "spoke" to you. Then, respond honestly to the questions and statements that follow.

Principle: _____

_____

Meaning/Significance:

_____

_____

_____

_____

Principle: _____

_____

Meaning/Significance:

_____

_____

_____

_____

Principle: _____

_____

Meaning/Significance:

_____
_____
_____
_____
_____

Principle: _____

_____

Meaning/Significance:

_____
_____
_____
_____
_____

Principle: _____

_____

Meaning/Significance:

_____
_____
_____
_____
_____

Principle: _____

_____

Meaning/Significance:

_____
_____
_____
_____
_____

Principle: _____
_____

Meaning/Significance:

_____
_____
_____
_____
_____

Principle: _____
_____

Meaning/Significance:

_____
_____
_____
_____
_____

Take a few minutes to think about your Personal Growth and Development and answer the following questions:

Have I done all that I could have done to accelerate or facilitate my Personal Growth and Development?

Yes_____ No_____

If not, why? (Be as specific as you can.)

_____

_____

_____

_____

What *specific* actions can I take now to help move me toward greater Personal Growth and Development? (List 4 or 5 items.)

_____

_____

_____

_____

How might my life be different in the future if I achieve the greatest level of Personal Growth and Development within my capacity? (Identify at least 5 examples.)

_____

_____

_____

_____

_____

How might my "thinking" be limiting my Personal Growth and Development? (Examine yourself deeply to find any possible answers.)

_____

_____

_____

_____

_____

Here are some people and resources that can help me with my Personal Growth and Development (Be wide-ranging in your thinking.)

_____

_____

_____

_____

_____

INTERPERSONAL
RELATIONSHIPS

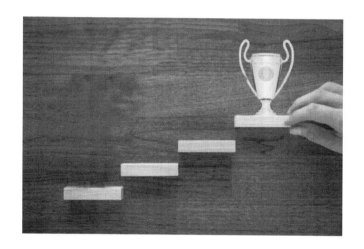

*You will never be "granted"
true friendship; you must earn
it through commitment, honor,
integrity and trust.*

I t is often said that, if you have one friend in a lifetime, you should consider yourself blessed. The word "friendship" is abused and overused. People try to buy friendship, to manipulate it, and to steal it. Some even assume that simply calling another person friend will make it so. But, the nature of true friendship is a clear, unspoken understanding between two people that transcends the value of money and does not need a physical presence to comfort and inspire. The understanding is based on a mutual sense of admiration, commitment, honor, honest and trust; and it is not measured by who owes what to whom. When you earn true friendship, the bearer expects nothing in return.

You won't go anywhere by making enemies.

Your reputation tends to precede you. If it is bad, it will not endear you to others, even when they don't know you personally. And, there is no faster way to give yourself a bad reputation than to show a sour disposition, or put others down, or make unkind comments and belittling statements. A bad reputation is a weapon of self-destruction. People will keep their distance and refuse to offer sound advice; they will not speak in your defense or willing to share information and resources. In the end, they might not purposely hurt you; but they purposely will not help you.

INTERPERSONAL RELATIONSHIPS

If you always look for the worst in others, you're likely to find it… even when it isn't there.

I t is curiously human for us to look for and conveniently find all manners of failings, faults and foibles in others. It seems that we'll look unyieldingly until we find them, but we can't seem to find or see them in ourselves. Maybe it is that our embellished opinions of ourselves lead us to believe others' personal attributes, characteristics and idiosyncrasies make them less than we and, therefore, unworthy of our consideration, respect and time. Moreover, if we expect others' personal attributes, characteristics and idiosyncrasies to be inferior to ours, we're likely to "see" them, whether they're evident or not.

If we earnestly look for the good in others, in spite of their human failings, faults and foibles, we are likely to find it.

What we think about others is probably what they think about us.

It is very easy to think our beliefs are correct and that others' beliefs are wrong. It is also very easy to make value for us to feel, self-righteously, that judgments about others based on our experiences and perspectives. It tends to be easy for us to harbor some rather negative beliefs and feelings about others because they are different from us. We can generate a roster of unkind names, or slap labels on them that tend to fit the images we create. What we often forget is that our beliefs, experiences, and perspectives are just that—ours.

We can't invalidate others or their beliefs, experiences and perspectives; and they cannot invalidate us or our beliefs, experiences and perspectives. The best that we can probably do is to listen to their beliefs, try to understand how they have experienced and are experiencing the world, and gain some insights into their perspective.

Hopefully, they will make the same effort to understand us. We mutually may learn that others probably don't see us the way we see ourselves.

*Everyone has a "Make-Me-Feel
Good" button; find it,
and then push it.*

D ifficult people are everywhere. They act as if they are angry with the world and seem to get their greatest enjoyment from being cantankerous, nasty and testy. Life would certainly be easier if we didn't have to deal with them, but sometimes we don't have a choice. However, if you look past the crusty, gruff exterior, you'll often find a kind and gentle person trying to get out. Look a little deeper and you'll usually find a person who wants to be understood, a person who wants to feel valued and worthwhile, a person who is usually burdened by many difficulties and misfortunes. Their difficult disposition is often a cry for help.

A gentle smile and a sympathetic ear can often help you escape the brunt of their wrath.

Don't make other people's problems yours; you will usually have enough of your own.

S ome individuals have a knack for feeding others their misery. They look for people on whom they can unload; people who will nurture their misery; people who have an empathetic and sympathetic ear. Those looking to unburden themselves become very good at talking about their misery, but they don't take any action to eliminate it. If you listen to them and internalize their misery, you too will be miserable and might even feel compelled to go and act for them, instead of helping them to act for themselves. If you do take on their problem, you will walk away feeling like somebody just put a thousand pounds on your back.

THEY DID!

If you spend all of your time meddling in other people's business, you won't have time to take care of your own.

It takes a lot of restraint not to try to solve other people's problems or to give them unsolicited advice, especially if you feel that you have better solutions and answers than they do. But, you have to remember that people act, behave, and think based on their own logic and rationale, which makes perfect sense to them, but totally illogical and irrational to you. Other people's faults, foibles, and problems are really no one else's business but their own.

Besides, taking care of your own business and attending to your own challenges and issues, if you're doing it properly, is a full-time job. And even working at it full-time most often will not guarantee success. So, how can you possibly take care of your business and still have time to meddle in the business of others? Still, many people try to do both, and they can't understand why they make so little progress in taking care of their own affairs.

Never dismiss people just because of their seeming lack of education, poor speech, or low social status.
You can often learn something valuable from them if you just take the time to listen.

Our knowledge is limited by our experiences. And, because we can't experience everything, we can't possibly know everything. That's why others' experiences can be invaluable in helping us to understand and interpret the world around us to some degree. By listening to them, we can understand how others experience and interpret the world and juxtapose that interpretation with our own.

To invalidate or dismiss that they have to share is much like destroying a fountain of knowledge. We are foolish to rely on their facility with the language as a barometer to gauge the value of what they say; or to calibrate their level of intelligence by observing how may letters they have after name.

Review all of the Interpersonal Relationship Principles and list at least four that had personal meaning and significance for you. Write what the Principle "spoke" to you. Then, respond honestly to the questions and statements that follow.

Principle: _____

_____

Meaning/Significance:

_____

_____

_____

_____

Principle: _____

_____

Meaning/Significance:

_____

_____

_____

_____

Principle: _____
_____

Meaning/Significance:

_____
_____
_____
_____
_____

Principle: _____
_____

Meaning/Significance:

_____
_____
_____
_____
_____

INTERPERSONAL RELATIONSHIPS

Principle: _____

_____

Meaning/Significance:

_____

_____

_____

_____

_____

Principle: _____

_____

Meaning/Significance:

_____

_____

_____

_____

_____

What are some Interpersonal Relationships that are preventing me from achieving my personal and professional dreams and goals, and what can I do to change those Relationships?

_____

_____

_____

_____

What are some Interpersonal Relationship that could help me to achieve my dreams and goals much faster, but I have avoided them because of my own "issues," such as my personal biases and beliefs about people who are not like me, fear of getting out of my comfort zone, and uncertainty of knowing how to act in certain social settings?

_____

_____

_____

_____

INTERPERSONAL RELATIONSHIPS

What are some Interpersonal Relationships from which I am constantly seeking something rather than contributing something, and what can I do to change that dynamic?

_____

_____

_____

_____

_____

What are some Interpersonal Relationships to which I am constantly giving but receiving nothing in return, and what can I do to change that dynamic?

_____

_____

_____

_____

PROFESSIONAL
DEVELOPMENT

An impressive résumé might get you in the door; after that you have to show what you can do.

Many people master the fine art of résumé writing. As mavens of the "how-to" phenomenon, they know the appropriate format, language, paper and style to use in order to attract attention. They also develop fine skills in garnering support and letters of references from colleagues, friends and former employers. They have developed superb techniques to get a prospective employer to give them the once-over. If they are fortunate enough to get an interview, they really turn on the charm and bolster it with a million-dollar look. They exude personality and style and certainly deserve praise for their efforts. However, there is something very important they often lose sight of:

An impressive résumé might get you in the door; after that you have to show what you can do.

Learn the written and unwritten rules of the game—then become the very best at playing by them.

There are many rules in life that we are expected to follow. We may not always like them, but they exist. Some are displayed or posted for all to see. These are "written" rules, and, because they are public knowledge, they are open to debate and discussion. Then there are other rules that are not public knowledge and that few people talk about; but some people seem to understand.

These "unwritten" rules, over time, have become an unspoken, but well understood, part of the social setting by those "in the know." These rules are just as important as, if not more important than, the written rules. Not knowing the unwritten rules will not make others forgive us for violating them.

Work hard and smart to become an expert at something; then use that knowledge and skills to get what you want.

"Expert" status is not something gifted, granted or willed; it is earned. One becomes an expert by striving to become the very best in an area of endeavor and choosing not to languish in mediocrity. Become an expert and many will seek your advice and council. Others will want to be associated with you and to share your preeminence. Be charitable with others, but be sure that you are rewarded for your efforts and expertise.

Don't get mad at the system; get motivated to work within to transform it; then act.

Systems exist to try to create some structure and semblance of order. They bring some sanity to what otherwise would be complete chaos. In many situations, however, a system exists solely because an attitude of "We've always done things this way" prevails. Nobody remembers why and apparently nobody is willing to challenge the status quo. A system like this can increase your level of frustration, raise your blood pressure a few points, and push your patience to the limit because you know it is defective, obsolete and useless and should be abandoned.

However, although a system may not always work the way you want it to, it can serve a useful purpose If it works for others, it probably can work for you too. You may have to ask a lot of "whys" in order to understand how it flows and what its functions and rationale is. But, if a system creates more chaos than order, suggest ways to change it.

Just don't sit and complain about it. Do something.

The person who is best positioned is the person with the superior information.

We place a high premium on information and its accuracy and timeliness. Information is being generated continuously. The real issue is: Who has access to it and how is it being used? The generators and purveyors of information traditionally have ensured that it remains in the hands of a select few who use it to their advantage and to the disadvantage of others. However, contrary to popular belief, the select few are not unusually capable, gifted or talented. They are individuals who share "insider trading" on Wall Street, or who hatch strategic plans in corporate boardrooms, or who debate local zoning changes.

In short, they are people who have access to the information and who are positioned to benefit from it personally, or who can ensure that their close circle of friends and supporters know about it. Those who are not in the flow of such information cannot benefit from it; in fact, in many instances, they will be hurt by not having the information in time to respond to it proactively. They remain in a reactionary state, one that forces them to play "catch up." As a result, they can't plan and strategize to work toward the results they would like to see.

The formula for success is to work hard and smart,
stay committed, be dedicated and focused,
and get rid of self-defeating and self-limiting attitudes and behaviors.

While your success is determined by how you define it, it is rarely achieved accidentally. The way you focus on success and set out to achieve it will determine the ultimate result. Many people dream about success and talk about it, but they make little or no effort to achieve it. It is as if they believe dreaming and talking will make success fall in their lap. However, their thinking goes, success is an unattainable goal on their own efforts, so why bother?

Then, there are those who will exert extraordinary efforts toward achieving their success, on the one hand, and who exhibit attitudes and behaviors that undermine their success on the other. It is as if they believe they don't really deserve the success they are striving to achieve. Their apparent fear of success is so daunting that it lessens their prospects of achieving it.

You can't achieve success with excuses;
success requires actions.

Y ou'll never have to look very hard to find excuses. In fact, some people become adept to using excuses to explain every conceivable circumstance. For example, they can always find some "legitimate" reason for not doing something they were supposed to do or had promised to do. These people can find convenient excuses for not accomplishing all the things in life that they want, and they fully expect others to continue accepting their excuses. They fail to realize that their excuse-finding is a waste of their and others' time. But, their excuse-finding, eventually, falls on unsympathetic ears. The message that others begin to hear clearly is: "I'd rather find reasons for not attempting to accomplish what I promised or set out to do than to make a concerted effort to try. And, I'm not really committed."

Review all of the Professional Development Principles and list at least three that had personal meaning and significance for you. Write what the Principle "spoke" to you. Then, respond honestly to the questions and statements that follow.

Principle: _____

_____

Meaning/Significance:

_____

_____

_____

_____

Principle: _____

_____

Meaning/Significance:

_____

_____

_____

_____

Principle: _____

_____

Meaning/Significance:

_____

_____

_____

_____

_____

Principle: _____

_____

Meaning/Significance:

_____

_____

_____

_____

_____

PROFESSIONAL DEVELOPMENT

Principle: _____

Meaning/Significance:

_____

_____

_____

_____

_____

Principle: _____

Meaning/Significance:

_____

_____

_____

_____

Some ways the Professional Development Principles will help me to approach and think about my Career/ Profession include:

_____

_____

_____

_____

_____

PRINCIPLES

Personal Growth and Development

1. Take personal responsibility for your actions and inactions.

2. If you don't believe in yourself, no one else will.

3. It is from our greatest challenges that we often discover our true strengths.

4. Don't go around picking up rocks and putting them in your wagon—they get heavy real soon.

5. If you don't think and act like a victim, you won't be one.

6. When you change your attitude, you can change your life.

7. If you have no goals, you're like a ship without a rudder.

8. The quality of our lives is determined by the choices we make.

9. You don't manage time; you can only manage yourself during the time you have.

10. Don't use others' prejudices as excuses for not achieving your goals; their prejudices are all the more reason for you to succeed.

11. The world owes you nothing; what you get out of life is in proportion to what you put into it.

12. You cannot let your current circumstances define who you are and what you are capable of becoming.

13. Manage your own expectations—positive and negative. Don't let others do it for you.

14. Do not become consumed by material possessions; they are not substitutes for accomplishments, attitude, competence, confidence, contribution and knowledge.

15. If we are lost in life, the best way to find ourselves is through serving others.

16. If you can't find peace and happiness within yourself, you're not likely to get it from others.

17. Very few worthwhile things in life are accomplished without dedication, pain, purpose and sacrifice.

18. Use every "Failure" as a learning experience, not as an excuse to give up.

19. Holding on to missed opportunities keeps us from seeing and acting on the next opportunities.

20. Growth and development is a never-ending journey, not a final destination.

21. It is better to have education and knowledge and not need it, than to need it and not have it.

Interpersonal Relationships

1. You will never be "granted" true friendship; you must earn it through commitment, honor, integrity and trust.

2. You won't go anywhere by making enemies.

3. What we think about others is probably what they think about us.

4. If you always look for the worst in others, you're likely to find it…even when it isn't there.

5. Everyone has a "Make-Me-Feel-Good" button; find it, and then push it.

6. Don't make other people's problems yours; you will usually have enough of your own.

7. If you spend all of your time meddling in other people's business, you won't have time to take care of your own.

8. Never dismiss people just because of their seeming lack of education, poor speech, or low social status. You can often learn something valuable from them if you just take the time to listen.

Professional Development

1. An impressive résumé might get you in the door; after that you have to show what you can do.
2. Learn the written and unwritten rules of the game—then become the very best at playing by them.
3. Work hard and smart to become an expert at something; then use that knowledge and skills to get what you want.
4. Don't get mad at the system; get motivated to work within to transform it; then act.
5. The person who is best positioned is the person with the superior information.
6. The formula for success is to work hard and smart, stay committed, be dedicated and focused, and get rid of self-defeating and self-limiting attitudes and Behaviors.
7. You can't achieve success with excuses; success requires actions.

About the Author

Dr. Wilbur Brower is the founder and president of W. Brower & Associates, a management consulting and training firm, specializing in human and organizational development. Dr. Brower is a former member of the U. S. Air Force and an executive with Bell Telephone Laboratories and AT&T, where he held numerous line and staff positions. He has consulted and trained for clients such as the AT&T, The University of Memphis, DuPont Pharmaceuticals, Dow Chemical Company, U. S. Veterans' Administration, Raleigh News and Observer, U.S. Army Corps of Engineers, U. S. Postal Service, National CASA and Illinois Youth Advocacy Programs. He also has been a guest lecturer at Fayetteville State University, University of Michigan, North Carolina Central University and Webster University, and a visiting professor with the National Urban League's Black Executive Exchange Program (BEEP).

He is also a retired high school Business Education and English teacher, and he is the founder and president of the Institute for Youth Development & Educational Resources (IYDER), Inc., a non-profit organization that provides training for students at-risk of academic and personal failures, and for educators who are struggling to understand and reverse academic underachievement among disadvantaged students. He has been a presenter at several national, state and regional conferences, including NC Dropout Prevention, NC Department of Public Instruction's Closing the Achievement Gap, At-Risk Youth National Forum, NC Communities in Schools, and Black Administrators in Child Welfare. He designed and developed STEP-UPP, a learning process for students at-risk of academic and personal failure; a companion learning process titled *The Teacher as Manager and Understanding and Reversing Academic Under-Achievement among Disadvantaged Students,* a learning process for teachers and administrators interested in closing the academic achievement gap.

Some of his writings on the subjects of organizational and personal effectiveness have appeared in *Harvard Business Review* (Nov.-Dec., 1996) and *Cultural Diversity at Work* (January, 1997). One of his major presentations was published in *Vital Speeches of the Day* (Feb 15, 2000).

A Little Book of Big Principles Values and Virtues for a More Successful Life

Wilbur L. Brower, Ph. D.

Made in the USA
Columbia, SC
22 December 2022

73653818R00072